MATOME LIPHY RAMALEPE

ONE THING

MATOME LIPHY RAMALEPE

ONE 1THING

REARABILWE AFRICA SOLUTIONS PTY LTD
Publishing, Leadership and Research Solutions

ISBN: 978-0-620-70086-3

Published by:

Rearabilwe Africa Solutions Pty Ltd

P O Box 2314

Tzaneen

0850

www.rearabilweafricasolutions.co.za

Acknowledgements

*N*o one can claim full credit of any measure of accomplishment in any endeavour in life. This book is no difference. The book is the result of corporate effort. Just as it takes a village to raise a child, so it took a team to author this book. I want to thank pastors, preachers, youth and women of our church 'Kingdom of Priests Assembly International' for their inputs, motivation and continued pursuit of me in getting the January message 'One Thing' published in this form. Your value surpasses that of jewels. This project could not have been completed without you.

Thank you all!

"Drawing from the inspiring message 'One Thing', the book urges us to have specific and right targets to desire. Most of the things we wish and pray for are the fruits of ONE THING - God's kingdom and his way of doing things (Matt 6:33)."

Pastor Peter Mahasha

"*One Thing* answers All things..."

Frederick Bill Mafa

"After the introduction of the message titled "One Thing", I felt the Holy Spirit continuing to minister in my life. Therefore, this book has the unique power to enlighten the congregation about the power of seeking one thing in order to locate our hidden treasures."

Tshepo Ramalepe

"I had been trying many things in life without success. I obviously missed 'one thing' that could have changed many things in my life."

Eric Mohale

"...It's only now that I realise that what I always thought was my 'one thing' isn't. And as I pray I understand there is one thing necessary that I need to put my mind to, which I haven't discovered."

Petunia Hlangwane

"When I heard the message "One thing" on the first Sunday of 2016, I told myself that this was not for me because I needed and wanted lots of things in my life not just "one thing". So, what is this "one thing"? In this book, Pastor Liphy Ramalepe explicitly describes one thing as that which is desirable, essential, and lacking.

Nthabiseng Maenetja

"Every 'one thing' bears fruits. Solomon's 'one thing' (wisdom) produced wealth, treasures and popularity."

Tshegofatso Pilusa

ONE THING

"One thing," says the sweet Psalmist,

"I desire," "That will I seek after"

Oh, Sweet Psalmist!

You seek after this one thing,

Like a deer that pants for water,

What is it? What is in it?

What is this 'one thing'?

Oh, Sweet Psalmist!

Just a fondness of heart?

Just a single wish?

Just a yen of a soul?

Nah!

But, affections bound up in one affection,

Sum of all your desires, and

All your desires molted into one mass,

Oh, Sweet Psalmist!

Seeing you would make but one request to God,

Why not make greater than this?

Why not repose and safety?

Why not tranquility?

Why not thousand other good things?

Why desire only to dwell in God's house?

What to do? But only to see?

And to see what?

but only a beauty?

at most but to enquire, what is enquiring?

but only to hear news about God?

O sweet Psalmist!

What goes with it?

What profit you promise yourself by it?

Mark, O my soul!

With the fixedness of thought on this,

With unwavering attention on this one thing,

with a holy flame of devout of affections,

with earnest covetousness,

you found true contentment,

having fixed you desire upon this one thing,

dwelling in God's house,

gazing the loveliness,

gazing the majestic grandeur of God,

you were assured of quietness and easiness,

in the Lord's house, you hid in secret,

there, troubles cannot reach you,

for you are set on high,

when you triumphed, you cheered,

and offered sacrifices of joy

All these benefits are yours,

Just by setting your heart on the pearl - One thing!

One thing, essential!

You desired it.

A rich young man lacked it.

Mary chose it.

Why, one thing?

Why narrow the wedge?

Share with me your discernment.

Does a man of many pursuits succeed?

Nah! Like Martha,

he gets worked up,

he becomes anxious about many things,

Then, discontentment and disappointment follow,

Distraction tags along behind,

Also I, knew, deeply inside,

One thing calls for discovery.

One thing David desired.

One thing Mary chose.

One thing a rich young man lacked.

Then, my soul whirled,

My mind murmured,

For my 'one thing'

ONE THING

Important Questions to Answer

What is the "ONE Thing" that is the aggregate of all the desires of your heart?

_____

What is the "ONE Thing" you can do such that by doing it everything else will be easier or inessential?

_____

What is the "ONE Thing" that stands between you and your goals?

_____

What is the "ONE Thing" lacking that makes your life void of peace, passion and purpose?

_____

ONE THING

David seeks after one thing because ...

"If you chase two rabbits, you will not catch either one"

Proverb

Mary chooses to dwell at Jesus' feet because ...

"We discover our true identity the more closely we are drawn to our Lord Jesus"

The Author

Apostle Paul forgets what lies behind because ...

"We all make mistakes, have struggles, and even regret things in our past. But you are not your mistakes, you are not your struggles, and you are here now with the power to shape your day and your future"

Steve Maraboli

TABLE OF CONTENTS

Introduction

"A new year is like a new chapter in my life waiting to be written, new questions to be asked, embraced, and loved. Answers to be discovered and then lived in this transformative year of delight and self-discovery. Today carve out a quite interlude for yourself in which to dream, pen in hand. Only dreams give birth to change."

(Author unknown)

It was a sun-drenched Friday morning, the first day of 2016. I got out of bed with a rekindled desire to change things in my life, family, and ministry in 2016. Every change begins with a dream, and every dream begins with a discovery. A point of departure in the process of discovery is asking and embracing new questions. Questions alone do not help the process if not accompanied by valid answers. When answers are discovered and accepted, self-discovery is attained. I thus began the journey of discovery with a single question from heart, "What dreams and desires are worth pursuing this year?" Surprisingly, the list was too long; it had countless desires, which included even unfulfilled dreams of 2015. It was therefore unimaginable that I could have all these desires fulfilled in just 366 days. The sum of all desires frustrated me. It challenged me to rethink my priorities.

While still reassessing my primary concerns for the year, the words of King David leaped out at me (Psalm 27:4). It seemed like God was giving me a direct encouragement that I would need only one thing (one desire) in order to change everything that stayed the same prior 2016. I then scrapped my list of dozen desires and dreams and focused on one thing. How do I identify this one thing out of the dozen other desires? How do I narrow the wedge? I asked myself. Reading Psalm 27:4, I was able to see King David's desire. But this was David's one thing, I needed to discover my own 'one thing'. Therefore, a new challenge arose from this passage of Scripture. This challenge necessitated a new struggle to discover my "One thing". This time the journey involved five set of questions, not just one as before:

What is one thing needful, that I can seek after, in order to change major things in my life?

If I were to express, at this moment, the one desire of my heart, what would it be?

What sincere and essential thing I have not done previously that if I had chosen to do things would be different today?

What one thing is lacking in my life, which I can earnestly covet, that if it were present I would not be where I am today?

If I were to forget one thing that happened in the past, what would it be?

These were questions from heart. I struggled to get answers to these five important questions the whole day. At around eight o'clock the next morning, I was still sitting with a long list of what seemed to be all my priorities. As a result, I got more and more frustrated. At around that time, my younger brother, Tshepo arrived while I was still battling to identify my one thing. Unconsciously, I said to him, "I think there is one thing I need to get this year, and if I get it, everything will change." I added, still inadvertently, "Yes, if I get a university job, I am gone, and many things would definitely change in my life. David's one thing is to dwell in God's house, but I think my one thing is to work at university this year." My younger brother nodded, smiled broadly with a smile of fascination, and said, "Ok! That's great!"

However, as I continued to provide answers to each of the five questions, immense uncertainty about regarding a university job as a needful thing to pursue engulfed my mind. How can a mere university job bring expected changes in my life? Is this an unrealistic dream? I asked myself despondently.

A resounding "yes" was a response to this question. Although the university job would provide limitless possibilities for my career as an academic, it would equally put a strain on my family and ministry. It would mean I have to travel long distances every week, and this would consume a lot of family and ministry time. Apart from all these obvious concerns about the university job, it was astonishing just how my mind could not completely discard it as my "one thing." This meant that a struggle to identify my one thing was far from over. The struggle itself snowballed. And it seemed identifying my "one thing" was like a mission impossible.

Yet, I was still convinced that focusing on one thing would give me unprecedented breakthroughs in 2016. I was then prompted to entitle our January series "One Thing". It is to a greater extent a tradition in our church to usher in every new year with a series commonly known as "The January Message". After introducing the message, members of our church persistently urged me to get the message published in the form of a booklet. At first, I was reluctant, but I finally bowed to pressure. I started writing, yet without clarity of which angle to consider in exploring the subject. However, several inputs and comments from members gave me a perspective. This perspective dramatically changed the object of writing this book from sharing our January message to providing the key characteristics of "one thing." The characteristics are drawn from four "one things" identified from the Bible. Therefore, the book is of an introspective nature assisting all of us to discover our one thing by answering four significant questions: "Is this one thing I ardently desire?", "Is this one thing necessary to pursue as a decided preference?", "Is this one thing lacking in my life?", and "Is this one thing to do to press towards the goal?" I hope that when I personally seek and find answers to these questions, you too may discover your one thing and have all your desires molten into one mass.

1

ONE THING

"Desired"

❝ **One thing I have desired** of the Lord, That will I seek: That I may dwell in the house of the Lord all the days of my life, To behold the beauty of the Lord, And to inquire in his temple"

Psalm 27:4

ONE THING

"A desire fulfilled is sweet to the soul"

(Proverbs 13:19a)

I f you were to ask but one thing to God, what would it be? What one thing do you have at heart more than anything? If you were to express the one thing of your heart, I mean that which is really and sincerely so, what would it be? I have no doubt that many of you would point to various things such as income, family comforts, temporal enjoyments and so on. You would, you think, be well content with these because happiness is generally regarded as consisting such things. These are indeed legitimate desires and God has promised to grant them. For "He grants the desires of those who fear him" (Psalm 145:19).

But David, like his son Solomon, never asked any of these things. Under his painful circumstances, it seems naïve for him not to ask for repose, safety and a thousand other good things. But no, David has set his heart on the pearl and left the rest. He says, "One thing," "I have desired of the Lord, That will I seek." The Sweet Psalmist teaches us that eminence and fulfillment come when we learn to pursue one desire that embodies everything we need. King David made a commitment to seek after his one desire. The word 'seek' is an action word that means to look for and find God, especially when this demands a lot of effort. This means getting our desires fulfilled is not effortless. To get it fulfilled, we have to seek after it, act on it, and pray about it.

ONE THING CALLS FOR RESOLUTE ACTIONS

No matter how holy and ardent a desire is, if it does not lead to resolute action it is just a wish. The old proverb says, "Wishers and woulders are never good housekeepers." To 'seek after' is to 'act on' the desire. Someone once said, "Desires are seed which must be sown in the good soil of activity or they will yield no harvest." We will find our desires to be like a cloud without water, unless followed up by practical endeavours. David realised that to tap into everything drenched in his one thing, he needed to commit to three important activities: to dwell, to behold, and to enquire. Having fixed his desire on the 'one thing' needful, he became active. He sought after his one thing, he continued to pray for it and contrived his affairs so as to have liberty and opportunity to get it. As a tripod stand gives a needed support to a telescope, the three activities provided a balance of life David needed during hard times.

Dwelling in God's house

David's one thing consisted of a commitment to dwell in the house of the Lord all the days of his life. For the sake of communion and fellowship with his God, David's prayer and objective is to be where the Lord is. Traditionally, the priests had their lodgings in the courts of God's house. King David tells us about his wish to leave the palace and be with the priests. As one of the greatest kings that ever was, he would have gladly desired to take his lodging with greatest men of this world, rather he desires to duly and constantly attend public service of God with other faithful Israelites. David's one thing involves a desire to reside permanently in the house of God and engage permanently in the service of the Lord. What a contrast is this to the conduct of Christians who attend church only occasionally, when the opportunity appears to them to favour it, or when worldly engagements do not interfere. Unlike most of us, the Psalmist attended church voluntarily without being coerced. He did not go to the house of God with improper motives, induced to come to show submission to authority, from a compliance with custom, or from the accusation of conscience. Attending church services should be a voluntary action, not an induced response.

4

Our church used to have a disappointing turnout for our Friday services. The turnout continued to vex me, especially considering that our church only had two normal meetings or services per week [one on Friday evening and another on Sunday morning.] I felt obliged to resort to confrontation and admonition. I thought rebuking and admonishing members was my only recourse in this situation. However, when I constantly confronted and rebuked members for not attending Friday services, the situation spiralled out of control. Members resisted and attendance continued to drop even further. I then became aware of the fact that a regular attendance at church services begins with a desire. It starts with affection for the house of the Lord. I believe that any child of God should always desire to come to church, to be passionate about fellowship with his or her heavenly Father and other saints.

Beholding God's beauty

The object of the psalmist's desire included to 'behold his beauty'. This means David attended the temple to gaze at the beauty of his God. The object of his desire was to see God, as he is. Strengths and beauty are in God's sanctuary (Psalm 96:6). To gaze at the beauty of the Lord is the exercise for both the earthly and heavenly worshippers. Both the heavenly and earthly worshippers are required to worship in the beauty of his holiness (Psalm 29:2). Now, what is God's beauty? God's beauty is his holiness (Psalm 110:3). God's beauty is his goodness (Zech 9:17). Beauty is simply the harmony of all the attributes of God's nature. We can call God's beauty the infinite and transcendent amiableness of the divine being and perfections. Therefore, to behold the beauty of the Lord is to see his holiness, to taste all his goodness, and to enjoy entirely what God is.

Therefore, the intent of entering our assemblies is not to see others, and be seen, or merely to hear the preacher, but rather to learn more of the loving Father, more of the glorious Jesus, more of the mysterious Spirit. As we behold his beauty, we more lovingly admire, and more reverently adore the trinity of God. To view the beauty of the Lord is to contemplate God's glories and excellencies, and entertain ourselves with tokens of his peculiar favour to us. This requires fixing our thought, having a holy flame of devout affections. We, therefore, need to enter God's house to enjoy God's divine presence in ordinances, to behold his beauty. The beauty of the Lord, that display of his presence and perfections which are made to the minds of his true and spiritual worshippers, is fully revealed when we seek after one thing – to dwell in the house of the Lord all the days of our lives. Our meetings on Sundays should be about beholding 'the King in his beauty' (Isaiah 6:1-3). This explains the purpose of attending church services.

Enquiring in God's temple

Finally, the object of David's earnest desire is to enquire in God's temple. The object of the Psalmist's ardent desire includes an obedient, diligent, and successful study of the divine will – to enquire in his temple. This simply means, as Pastor Mahasha puts it, 'to gather information about God and his divine will." We must find satisfaction of being instructed in our duties, instructed about God's will for our lives, and concerning this we should come to church as enquirers. A church service should, therefore, become an enquirers' meeting. We must go there to enquire about the perfect will of God for our lives. We must also enquire how we maybe more assured of God's will. We shall not need to make enquiries in heaven, for there we shall know even as we are known, but we should in the meantime sit at Jesus' feet and awaken all our faculties to learn of him. Enquirers are inquisitive people. Nothing passes without them asking questions about it. They find pleasure in knowing the activities of their God, because their God is constantly at work.

SEEKING AFTER 'ONE THING' DESIRED

The word "seek after" most probably means 'to come morning by morning', 'to frequent God's presence, giving him the beginning of each day.' Some of us will never receive our other desires until we change our attitudes towards church. We will not receive our breakthroughs until we decide to commit ourselves to the house of God. Our advancement in life is in our decision to live all the days of our lives in God's presence, to behold his beauty, and to enquire in his house. To do these three things, however, may mean that we must make major changes in our thinking and lifestyle. We need to be willing to change our values in order to know Christ better. We need to fix and rearrange our crowded schedule in order to set aside a few minutes each day for prayer and Bible study. We need to prioritise time for church services. We need to change some of our plans, goals and desires in order to conform with what we learn about Christ. Whatever we must change or give up, dwelling in the house of God and enquiring there will be more than worth the sacrifice.

THE BENEFITS OF SEEKING AFTER ONE THING

Any good practice generates good profits. There are also profits of dwelling in God's house to gaze at his beauty and enquiring about him. There are obvious benefits recorded in Psalm 27. I believe that what made David steadfast in serving his God was the understanding of the benefits of doing so. By dwelling in the house of the Lord, we are guaranteed safety and security. There is protection in David's one thing. When enemies become armies and enmity open warfare, God becomes our shelter. When we are in his presence, he keeps us secure from the darkness of surrounding trouble. God is our stronghold, a place where our lives dwell in safety.

We, like David, we face people bent on evil, full of savagery and hostility, but it is in this situation that we find protection flowing from our one thing. God lifts us up on a high rock, a place of inaccessible safety, a place where the raging threatening billows of a stormy sea cannot touch us. He sets us up upon a rock which will not sink under us. On this rock, we find firm footing for our hopes. God is a protector of our exposed life. He keeps us from being slain, and keeps us from fainting, sinking, and dying away. God's protection results in personal triumph. David says his head shall be exalted above the enemies around him. Not only does God sets us on a rock higher than us so as our enemies cannot reach us with their darts, but also so that we shall be exalted to bear rule over them. This means that there is a personal victory in his one thing. With an undaunted courage, he triumphed over his enemies. His enemies came upon him to eat up his flesh, aiming at no less, but God smote them and fell. They were so confounded and weakened that they could not go on with their enterprise.

Because of this personal triumph, David enthusiastically states that he will offer the sacrifices of praise. Whenever we overcome our foes, the house of the Lord turns into a place of cheerfulness and pleasantness. Whatever is the matter of our joy ought to be the matter of our praise. When we attend church, we ought to be much in joy and praise. It is for the glory of God that we should sing in his way, and, whenever God lifts us up above our enemies, we ought to exalt him in our praises.

2

ONE THING

"Essential"

"As they continued their travel, Jesus entered a village. A woman by the name of Martha welcomed him and made him feel quite at home. She had a sister, Mary, who sat before the master, hanging on every word he said. But Martha was pulled away by all she had to do in the kitchen. Later, she stepped in, interrupting them,. "Master, don't you care that my sister has abandoned the kitchen to me? Tell her to lend me a hand." The master said, "Martha, dear Martha, you're fussing far too much and getting yourself worked up over nothing. **One thing is essential**, and Mary has chosen it – it's the main course, and won't be taken from her"

(Luke 10:38-42).

ONE THING

"Contentment and fulfillment are by-products of the process of discovering something essential in life"

L ife is a voyage of discoveries. We discover new facts and new truths about our own world. We discover answers when wrestling with tricky questions and controversies of life. We discover viable solutions to real-life problems. Most importantly, we discover ourselves. In Luke 10:38-42, Jesus introduces us to a discovery made by a woman called Mary. When Martha rudely complained to him about her lazy sister, he replied gently and firmly, "One thing is essential [worth being concerned about], and Mary has chosen [discovered] it." Mary discovered a valuable treasure at the feet of Jesus. What Mary discovered was of an ultimate value to her life.

What happens when you discover a hidden treasure, it may be of antique or archaeological value such as gold? Certainly, you would do exactly what Mary did – stay at the discovery site. Jesus compares the kingdom of God with a treasure that a man discovered hidden in a field. What does he do? He says, "In excitement, he hid it again and sold everything he owned to get enough money to buy the field" (Matthew 13:44). You see, any treasure you discover in life is worth selling everything you have to own it. Mary found that nothing compares to the joy, fulfillment, and significance of discovering one thing that is as essential as residing at the discovery point. She is mentioned three times in the Gospel account. Every time she is mentioned, she is found at the discovery site, at the feet of Jesus. She was ready to surrender everything she once valued so she may be with Jesus. She sold her time to buy time with Jesus. She sold her relationship with her sister to buy relationship with Jesus.

PRIORITIES: MARTHA LABOURED, MARY LISTENED

Looking in on this scene at Martha's home, we can tell what each sister's priorities were. Martha's prime concern was in preparing an elaborate supper to serve and impress her guests. Mary, however, was more concerned with being at the feet of Jesus. While Martha laboured, Mary listened. While Martha tried her best to be a good hostess, Mary tried her best to be a good listener. To me, the story presents a constant war between nonessentials and essentials. Martha found it difficult to detach herself from nonessentials to concentrate on the essentials. Mary, on the other hand, detached herself from nonessentials to engage in what is essential. Then, Jesus came in to clarify to Martha an important activity that Mary

13

prioritised. He calls this activity 'one thing'. To help Martha to get clarity on the essential things, he introduces the law of priority. Within the context of this story, the law of priority would state 'Some things are prime concerns meriting attention before their competing alternatives.'

By stating 'one thing is essential', Jesus implied that some things have status of being prior and should take precedence based on their importance. Even though food is necessary to physical life, Jesus teaches us that excessive attention to the kitchen may keep a person from experiencing even more important spiritual food. The story teaches us that service to Jesus must not fill our lives to such an extent that we have no time to learn from him. Too often, we are more like Martha than like Mary. In our zeal to serve the Lord, we wind up ignoring him. Too often, we fail to prioritise spending time with him. Eventually, we get ourselves pulled away from him. It is important to remember that we honour him more by listening to him than by providing excessively for his needs. By listening to him, we proof to be his sheep (John 10:3).

Jesus states, "Mary has chosen it [one thing]." This implies that prioritising is ability to make a choice between two competing alternatives. Contrasting the two sisters' activities, Jesus contrasts a concern over many things with the concern for one activity that matters. To me, Martha was not wrong to open her home for Jesus and serve him. In fact, Scripture condones hospitality. The challenge could have been that she was elaborate when a simple meal could have sufficed. On the other hand, Mary was not wrong to forsake the kitchen and open her heart to learn from Jesus. Both the gestures were correct according. Now, how to prioritise when everything seems to be a priority? The truth is, oftentimes, everything that we have to do seem like a priority, which makes it tough to figure out where to begin. It is easy to get overwhelmed when the to-do list consists of these kind of activities. Zooming into the story of the two sisters, I learned one simple strategy to choose between two competing alternatives. Jesus said, 'one thing is essential' to mean that effective prioritisation involves assessing the value of the task or activity before undertaking it. It simply means that doing or completing certain activity will offer more benefits than the other will. I have a golden rule that says 'God's agenda first, my personal agenda last." This is simply because neglecting God's work has often proved to have bigger ramifications than my personal staff. By saying, "One thing is essential, Mary has chosen it," Jesus meant that Mary was able to assess the value of sitting at the feet of Jesus as compared to spending her time in the kitchen.

15

THE BENEFITS IN MARY'S ONE THING

Some activities take precedence in our lives because of the benefits they offer us. Sitting at Jesus' feet granted Mary the exciting benefits. Some of the benefits of sitting at Jesus' feet that we can enjoy are that in Jesus' presence:

a. We become more and more like him

Often the level of spirituality we are able to achieve is related to the time we are willing to spend in his presence. The story of Moses teaches us how spending time in God's presence affects our spirituality. The Bible records that Moses was on the mountain with God for forty days and forty nights without eating bread or drinking water (Ex 34:28). When Moses came down from Mount Sinai, he was not aware that his face had become radiant because he had been with the Lord. God's divine presence and revelation changed Moses' appearance. He became more like his God. The more time we spent with God, the more we become like him. Prayer and fasting bring us closer to our God. Moses' closeness to God brought a radiance the people could not bear (Ex 34:29).

Our intimacy with God gives us a shining face the devil and his agents cannot bear. Our spiritual closeness with God makes Satan tremble. He trembles because whenever he sees us he sees God. Spending time with God in prayer brings identity to God's people. If everything in our lives takes precedence over being with the Lord, then we are in danger of losing our identity. Even being overly busy in his work, to a point where we have no time to spend at his feet, is a bad thing. The more time we spend at his feet, in his presence, the easier to make it a priority of life. Mary made this her priority. Is sitting at Jesus' feet a priority to you? Is this your 'one thing'?

b. We get instructions about the plans of life

Just as we need a plan to build a house, so to build a life, we also need to have a plan. We cannot just drift along and let life happen to us. We cannot just live aimlessly. Like any good artisan, we need a solid blueprint to guide us in life. Where do we get this blueprint? Where do we obtain this life plan? God is the Master Planner and his plans are always pregnant with grace. He says "For I know the plans I have for you," "They are plans for good not disaster, to give you a future and a hope." (Jeremiah 29:11). Our Master Planner knows the future, and his plans for us are for prosperity. As long as God, who knows the future, provides our agenda or plan of life, we can have

17

boundless hope that we will fulfill his mission and live purpose-driven life.

However, the crucial question is, "If God has good plans to proper us and to give us the future we expect, why are the majority of Christians not prospering as God would love us to? Perhaps, the straightforward answer I can offer is that "God's plans materialise when it is revealed and implemented." The Master Planner does not just meander seeking to reveal his plans to his people. Hence, James 4:8 urges, "Draw near to God and He will draw near to you." The elusive secret is that God reveals his plans when we are closer to him. In the forty days and forty nights that Moses spent in God's presence, God revealed so many plans, from plans for the Ark of the Covenant to plans for the construction of the Tabernacle.

Interestingly, God said to Moses, "Set up the tabernacle according to the plan shown you on the mountain" (Ex 26:30). 'According to the plan' means according to the direction corresponding to its meaning and purpose God unveiled about the tabernacle. We prosper when we live life according to the plan showed to us. We get this plan of life in God's presence. In addition, during Moses' stay on the mountain, God gave him instructions concerning the way in which Israel was to worship him through sacrifices, offerings and ceremonies. God prescribed the way in which he wanted Israel to approach him.

It is easy for people who spend time in God's presence to understand how God expects them to worship him. They get to understand that they do not approach and worship God in their own terms, but they have to approach him obediently in the way he prescribes. The longer time you spend in God's presence, the clearer the plans God has for you, your family and ministry become.

God, like in the days of Israel, has provided the people with a church as a holy place of worship which symbolises his continual presence with them. The church is not only a place of prayer and public worship to God, but also a place where God reveals his plans to individuals through his servants, the pastors. Therefore, people should change their attitude towards fellowship meetings in the church. To neglect Christian meetings is not only to give up the encouragement and help of other Christians, but it is also to give up the revelation of God's plans for your life. As we get closer to the day when Christ will return, people will face spiritual struggles and difficulties. But difficulties should never be excuses for missing church services. Rather, as difficulties arise and our struggles increase, we should make an even greater effort to be faithful in attendance.

c. We forget our cares

The larger Jesus gets in our eyes, the smaller other things become. The more he is magnified the more we forget about our cares. The more he increases the more life's anxieties, desire for riches and pleasure, which suffocate many people, decrease. While Martha was distracted, Mary was sitting calmly at Jesus' feet listening to his words. She cared less about hunger or whatsoever. When we come into his presence in prayer, praise and worship or bible study, the burdens of this present life grow amazingly light. Imagine having to worry about nothing! It seems like impossibility. We all have worries in our homes, in our jobs, at school, in our ministries. But Mary's story teaches us that if we want to worry less, we must spend more time at the feet of Jesus. It is here where we can turn our worries into prayers. Therefore, whenever you start to worry, run into the presence of the Lord. In his presence, we are bound to forget all our anxieties, all our concerns, as we cast them on him who cares for us – Christ our precious Saviour (1Peter 5:7).

d. We are spiritually nourished

As Martha was worried about physical nourishment, Marry was concerned about her spiritual nourishment. Like a newborn baby not letting go of the mother's breast, Mary hung on every word that Jesus said. Peter says that "Like newborn babies [you should] long for the pure milk of the word, so that by it you may be nurtured and grow in respect to salvation [its ultimate fulfillment]" (1 Peter 2:2 TAB). Those who crave for pure spiritual milk stay where the spiritual breast is – in the presence of the Lord. Remember, Christians are not born fully grown. They are like newborns that need to grow and mature. They grow and mature when they are spiritually breast-fed. To 'grow and mature' means progressing toward moral and spiritual perfection. The progression toward moral and spiritual perfection is a process that begins and ends with sanctification through God's word. Jesus prayed that the Father would separate his disciples from worldliness and dedicate and equip them for service (John 17:17). God's word, both written and spoken is the chief means by which God sanctifies us. Thus, the word of God fulfils the purpose of God to make us different from the world and make us holy. The more we drink the milk of the word, the more we become different from the world. Therefore, at Jesus' feet, Mary found food for her soul.

e. We find contentment and fulfillment

At Jesus' feet, Mary discovered the secret of contentment. Contentment is being self-sufficient in Christ. This is a sense of being satisfied to the point where you are not disturbed or uneasy regardless of circumstances. It is not easy to be content with whatever you have if you don't spend time in the presence God. God is El-Shaddai, the God who is more than enough (Exodus 6:1-6). When we feel empty inside, God fills any empty space in our lives. Paul says godliness is a source of great gain when accompanied by contentment (1Timothy 6:6). In Philippians 4:11, he says he has learned the secret of contentment whatever circumstances. He says he is happy with little as with much, with much as with little. Therefore, brothers and sisters, in sitting at the Lord's feet, we find something that millions live their entire lives and never discover. We find acceptance and true contentment, two things worth spending time for in God's presence. How can you find true contentment? The answer lies in your perspectives, priorities, and your source of satisfaction.

f. We discover our weaknesses

At Jesus' feet, we also discover our weaknesses and iniquities (Isaiah 6:1-6). Seeing the Lord and listening to the praises of the angels, Isaiah realised that he was sinful before God, with no hope of measuring up to God's standard of holiness. However, when his lips were touched with a live burning coal, he became pure. In response, Isaiah submitted himself entirely to God's service. The painful cleansing process is necessary before we can fulfill the task to which God is calling us. Before we accept God's call to represent him on earth, we must be cleansed as Isaiah was, confessing our sins and submitting ourselves to God's will. Therefore, at Jesus' feet, we are purified so that we can truly represent God, who is pure and holy.

3

One thing

"Lacking"

❝Now as he was going out of the road, one came running, knelt before him, and asked him, "good teacher, what shall I do that I may inherit eternal life?" ... you know the commandments: 'do not commit adultery', 'do not murder', 'do not steal', do not bear false witness', 'do not defraud', 'honor your father and your mother.'" and he answered and said to him, "teacher, all these things I have kept from my youth." Then Jesus, looking at him, loved him, and said to him, "**one thing you lack**: go your way, sell whatever you have and give to the poor, and you will have treasure in heaven, and come, take up the cross, and follow me." But he was sad at this word, and went away sorrowful, for he had great possessions"

(Mark 10:17-22).

24

ONE THING

"Generosity is a test of love and faith most people fail miserably"

Have you ever worried about whether or not you really are a Christian? Have you ever been in a situation that made you doubt your salvation? A rich young man found himself in this dilemma. The young man said he had never broken any of the laws Jesus mentioned. Perhaps he had even kept the Pharisees' additional regulations as well. Yet, he was still uncertain about inheriting eternal salvation. He thus came to Jesus in order to be sure God was pleased with him and would get the eternal blessings of his kingdom. So, he asked, "What shall I do to inherit eternal life [that is, eternal salvation in the Messiah's kingdom?" Jesus lovingly broke through the man's pride with a challenge that brought out his true motives: "Go your way, sell whatever you have and give to the poor, and you will have treasure in heaven, and come, take up the cross, and follow me." (Mark 10:21).

The more I read this passage, the more it kept me thinking. The more I thought about it, the more I asked myself this introspective question daily "Is there any barrier that could keep me out of the kingdom?" The young man went on with life unaware of an obstacle that stood between him and the kingdom of God. It seems so obvious from the statements of Jesus and the ultimate reaction of this young man that the young man's barrier was his love of money. His love of money was tantamount to idolatry. The greatest sin in the Bible by far is the sin of idolatry. Idolatry is when we put something or someone first in our life, before the living and true God. God commanded that "You shall have no other gods before me" (Exodus 20:3). This rich man, like many others loved his possession so much that it became his god. Money became the god that represented his pride of accomplishment and self-effort. Jesus had affection for this young man. He wanted him to be one of his disciples. He wanted him to inherit his kingdom. But a rich man found himself illegible for all these blessings because he had another god that ruled over his life. No wonder Jesus instructed him to go kill his god in order for him to qualify to carry the cross and follow him.

The story of this rich man teaches us that it is possible to observe most of the kingdom principles, and still miss certain kingdom benefits because of something or someone that has become our god. Jesus once said, "No one can serve two masters. For you will hate one and love the other, you be devoted to one and despise the other. You cannot serve both God and money" (Matthew 6:24). Money mastered this young man's life and dominated his life. Jesus was not condemning money itself. He condemned the man's obsession with money. Obsession with money is dangerous. It often makes people give greatest thought and priority on the money. It also develops into anxiety, making people troubled over the unknown tomorrow. People obsessed about money always want to make a lot of money today because they are worried about tomorrow. They will by hook or crook try to enrich themselves very quick. This is the reason we have so much corruption happening in our country. Politicians are worried about tomorrow, when their terms of office end. Their obsessional behaviour about money makes them temper with procurement processes, soliciting bribes from desperate entrepreneurs.

How would you react if God told you that the barrier keeping you from receiving eternal blessings is idolatry? How would you react if God reveals that your wealth has turned into idolatry? How would you react if the Holy Spirit told you that your obsession with your job has turned into idolatry? How would you respond if Jesus told you that your spouse has drawn you away from him? Will you get mad at him and leave his church? When Jesus confronted the rich man and revealed to him that he lacked one thing, his face clouded over. This was the last thing he wanted to hear, and he walked off with a heavy heart. He was holding tight on his money. He was not about to let go. If you put money before God, you will get sad if people tell you to offer it.

Generosity is a test of love and faith a young man failed miserably. Most of us, like the rich young man, have failed the test of generosity because we fail to understand that we are stewards of God's resources, including money. We fail to grasp that generosity is an act of love. This act is based on the principle, "And though I bestow all my goods to feed the poor, and though I give my body to be burned, but have no love, it profits me nothing" (1Corinthians 13:3). We fail the test of generosity by failing to recognise that generosity is an act of faith based on the trust that "It is more blessed give than to receive" (Acts 20:35). Giving to the poor should be driven by faith – the confidence on the sure words, "Whoever is generous to the poor lends to the Lord." Giving with faith is giving with an assurance that in due time God will repay us every cent we gave to the poor.

ONE THING LACKING: A GENEROUS HEART

Jesus said to the rich young man, "You lack one thing: Go, sell all that you have and give to the poor." Literally, Jesus was saying to this young man, "You want treasure in heaven? Be generous with your earthly treasure." We are told in Proverbs

22:9 that "He who has a generous eye will be blessed, For he gives of his bread to the poor." (Proverbs 22:9). It is clear here that one thing the rich man lacked in his life is a generous eye. A generous eye is an eye that sees the needy and provide for their needs. A generous eye can only be found in caring people, people who enjoy helping the poor.

In many respects, the attitude of many of us is quite similar to the attitude of this rich young man. We need inward blessings but we lack inward caring attitude. We expect God to consider us for his kingdom blessings, yet we ourselves are inconsiderate of the poor in his kingdom. We can only receive kingdom blessings when we take care of the poor. Like a magnet, a caring attitude attracts both spiritual and material blessings. When a caring attitude is translated into caring actions for people in need, it releases God's blessings. Jesus thus told the wealthy young man to go and commit his wealth to meet the needs of poor people. Such commitment removes wealth as an obstacle to receiving God's eternal blessings. For this young man a test of his faith was to do an act of mercy because Christ himself commanded it. Jesus exposed a barrier that could keep this young man out of the Kingdom - the love of money. Money represented his pride, pride of accomplishment and self-effort. It is God who gives us strength to accumulate wealth (Deuteronomy 8:18), so we must honour him with it (Proverbs 9:3).

Do you have one thing lacking that can keep you from receiving spiritual and material blessings? The rich young man lacked one thing – to sell all he had and give to the poor. Like this young man, people often fail to recognise that stewardship involves more than giving regular gifts to our local churches or God's work in general. It involves a caring attitude accompanied by the act of giving to the poor. Sometimes we are satisfied with paying tithe and giving offerings to our local assemblies, but before God, this is not enough. He still sees that one thing is lacking. He sees that we lack one thing - a generous heart in order to unlock our blessings, both spiritual and material.

Christians need to recognise that we serve God by serving people in need (Matthew 25:34-46). Christ's teachings on generosity always drawn people's attention to the least of this world (the widows, orphans, aliens, and the poor). In Matthew 25:34-46, Jesus virtually says to see him we must recognise him in the hungry, thirsty, strangers, sick, and imprisoned around us. If we say we love him, then we must love him through these oppressed humans.

BENEVOLENCE: PRACTICAL ACT OF LOVE

Late in 2014, I preached a two-month series entitled "The power of Giving." When addressing a sub-topic 'Love Driven Givers,' I said, "Love is action, action demonstrated through giving. Love is not complete without giving. God so loved the world, and he gave." In my introduction of this message, I explored John 21:15-17. I illustrated to the church how each time Peter stated that he loved Jesus, Jesus told him, "Feed my lambs," "Feed my sheep," and again, "Feed my sheep." Jesus was actually saying to Peter, practical acts of love are more than words. If you really love me, show it by actions – Feed my sheep. John espoused, "If anyone has material possessions and sees his brother in need but has no pity on him, how can the love of God be in him? Dear children, let us not love with words or tongue but with actions and in truth" (John 3:17, 18). If we see a person in an obvious need and say be clothed and warmed, but do not give to his or her need, God's love does not dwell in us.

Love manifests itself in generous giving. Like the rich young man, most of us claim we love God, but our love is not practical. First century believers had such powerful love that they claimed nothing as their own but sold their goods and gave the money to care for the needs of other believers (Acts 4:32-35). The rich young man came to ask Jesus what he could do to inherit the kingdom, but he left seeing what he was unable to do. One thing he has not done was giving to the poor. He shut his ears to the cries of the poor, and his own cries went unheard and his prayers unanswered (Proverbs 21:13). Hence, he came to find out what was wrong; he knew he was about to miss eternal blessings. When Jesus revealed that he lacked one thing, his true motives were exposed. He valued possessions above God. He loved his money. Paul says the love of money is the root of all kinds of evil (1Timothy 6:10a). Rich people craving greater riches are always caught in an endless cycle that only ends in ruin and destruction. Being benevolent is one of the key ways of avoiding the love of money (1Timothy 6:6-10). One thing that had kept me from the love of money is freely sharing what I have with others. Arguing against the love of money, I once said, "Money is the answer to everything" (Ecclesiastes 10:19c), but I don't love it, I need it. I need it to answer all things in my life. I also need it to answer all things in the lives of others, especially, the poor. If it makes my world go around, it must also make the poor's world go around. Do you love money or need it? Just as you cannot share your wife with anybody because you love her, so you cannot share money with anybody if you love it. If you love money, it is your god. But if you need it, you will share it.

THE PURPOSE AND BENEFITS OF GENEROSITY

It is impossible to read epistles of James 1: 27 and 1 john 3:17-18 without recognising that to help others in need is a true religion and it is an evidence of love. Therefore, one thing most people lack is expressing practical acts of love to show concern for the needs of others. I am so blessed to live in an area where interdenominational churches still meet to fellowship during Easter and Christmas. Our area is further blessed to have two powerful evangelists, Peter Makwala and Steve Maowasha, who are amazingly gifted in preaching about the subject of tithe and offerings. These servants of God are able to handle this subject with boldness, dissecting Scripture with accuracy to reveal to God's people the purpose and benefits of giving.

In one of our meetings, Evangelist-Pastor Peter Makwala read Proverbs 11:24 and bravely said, "Poverty is a choice. Prayer does not get rid of poverty, but giving does." What a bold statement! In this statement, I found a reason to argue that many of our spirit-filled, tongue-talking brothers and sisters live and die in their poverty because they have chosen to do so. I know this may sound like I am being insensitive. I personally believe that poverty is a curse, a curse we must eradicate through giving. You might be asking yourself, "What to give when I am dirt poor?" The Bible shows that you do not have to be rich to give to God something he will value. Basing his sermon "And a poor woman came" on Mark 12:41-44, Pastor Peter Mahasha said, "Poverty is not an excuse to give, because even a poor woman came and gave." He added, "God valued the widow's gift because not only she was poor, but was truly needy. Those two coins were all she had, and when she put them in the box, there was nothing left." This is what I call sacrificial giving. Sacrificial giving is simply parting with what you would rather keep. Sacrificial giving is a kind of giving that makes no human sense. Those who say they are poor so they cannot give are wrong because even a poor woman came and gave. I know a sacrificial gift is one that isn't easy to give, but once we give it poverty flies out of our lives for good. Remember, Jesus Christ, rich as he was, he gave it all away for our sake, in one stroke he became poor and we became rich (2 Corinthians 8:9). If for our sake, Jesus became poor, so that by his poverty we may become abundantly blessed, why are we still poor? We are poor because we fail to understand that the only way we can tap into his riches is through generosity. Therefore, the merit of generosity is to eliminate poverty, and help us reclaim our position as the heirs of the economically stable kingdom – the kingdom of God. Generosity brings the blessings of God to meet our economic and spiritual needs.

In 2 Corinthians 9:12-14, Paul mentions several other benefits of generosity. First, Paul shows that generosity goes much further than meeting physical needs. It draws people to God by the physical expression of Christian love. Second, our giving generates praises for God in other places from unknown people. As the result of our offerings, the recipients of our gifts will give glory to our God. Third, our generosity also leads people benefiting from our gifts to pray for us. There are some common words that people usually say when they see us going to church, 'Remember us in your prayers', or simply 'Pray for us'. But Paul teaches us that giving is the best way to get people remember you in their prayers. In fact, you don't have to request them to pray for you, moved by your offering, they will respond for you in a passionate intercession for whatever you need.

4

ONE THING

"Forgetting the past"

"Not that I have already obtained this or am already perfect, but I press on to make it my own, because Christ Jesus has made me his own. Brothers, I do not consider that I made it my own. But **one thing I do:** forgetting what lies behind and straining forward to what lies ahead, I press on toward the goal for the prize of the upward call of God in Christ Jesus"

(Philippians 3;12-14)

ONE THING

"Forget the past and pursue the future"

L ife is a race. Wreaths of victory await athletes who get to the finishing line. More than twice in his writings, Apostle Paul employs an illustration from the realm of athletics to demonstrate what it takes to win a race. First, he says, "Now every athlete who [goes into training and] competes in the games is disciplined and exercises self-control in all things" (1Corinthians 9:25). Second, "And if anyone competes as an athlete [in competitive games], he is not crowned [with the wreath of victory] unless he competes according to the rules (2 Timothy 2:5). Thirdly, he states that "...But one thing I do: forgetting what lies behind and straining forward to what lies ahead." (Philippians 2:12-14).

Drawing from the metaphor of athletics employed in the three passages we can easily discover three important requirements for winning the race. First, if we want to win the race we need personal discipline, the ability that results in a calm, well-balanced mind and self-control. Here, Paul draws imagery from the athletic events of the famous Isthmian games held near Corinth. He reminds them of the strict dietary and training discipline athletes in these events underwent in order to gain a crown. Second, to win the race we need to abide by the rules of the game. An athlete who trains extremely hard, but does not follow the rules will be disqualified. For example, if a competing athlete trains hard but on the day of the competition makes a "false start" (running before the starter's gun is fired), he can eventually be disqualified. If a hard training runner joggles a fellow athlete or tries to impede his progress by blocking, shoving to gain unfair advantage, the runner will be disqualified. Life is a race of rules. Those who fail to abide by its rules are never crowned. Third, if we are to succeed in this race of life we must very deliberately "forget", and very deliberately "press on." Paul says he does not consider himself a winner yet. But one thing he does, he does not look back, he lengthen his stride, he run straight toward the goal to win the prize. This is the most important requirement, without which the first two cannot be sustained. An athlete who constantly looks back during the race can easily impede others or run outside prescribed lane, leading to a disqualification. In addition, looking back is an obvious sign that an athlete lacks self-discipline. A disciplined runner keeps his eye on the goal. If we are to win the race, we need to run along the prescribed course, banishing all thoughts of past failures, and stretching every nerve in an effort of tremendous concentration on reaching our goal. Our one and only concern is to win the race.

ONE THING: FORGETTING THE PAST

In pronouncing, "One thing I do: Forgetting what lies behind...," Paul openly communicated his priorities as an athlete in a race of life. He narrowed his wedge and focused on one thing essential. What was his secret? He discerned what hindered him – the past. He had to let go of all things he once cherished, considering them distractions in the race. If we are to win any race in life, we need a single-minded passion [One thing], that is to forget the past and pursue the prize that lies ahead. It is sometimes crucial not to only forget our past failures; but also forget our past trophies as well, as long as they sidetrack us. Counting all the trophies and failures of our past as nonsense compared to the ultimate prize lying ahead is a good thing to do. Nothing hold people back than their past.

Hence, Isaiah says that we should not dwell in the past or ponder the things of the past (Isaiah 43:17-19). God wants us to forget about our past. He wants us to forget it all – all the oppression, pain, all the rejection, all the setbacks, all the despair, all the anger, all the failures of the past. He is about to do something new. In fact, he has already begun. He is making a pathway through the wilderness and creating rivers in the dry wasteland. He, however, asks, "See, I have already begun! Do you not see it?" (Isaiah 43:19). The reason we don't see it is because we are still holding on to our past. We keep carrying wounds from the past because we are scared of who we will become without them. Our past is blinding our minds from seeing the potential for bigger things in the future. God is doing a new thing, so let us start all over and fully partake in this grace. Let us let the past wither and die. For our past is a hindering factor, standing between the new thing and us. No wonder Paul asserts that getting the prize that lies ahead at the finishing line starts with doing one thing – forgetting the past. It is clear that our past has the power to suck the energy out of us, and we eventually fail to press on toward the goal. Our desire to press on to possess the future is fueled by the future that lies ahead, not the history that lies behind. Breaking the mighty cords tying us to our past is the first step in reclaiming our future.

PAUL'S REASONS TO FORGET THE PAST

Paul had reasons to forget the past. He had held the coats of those who had stoned Stephen, the first Christian martyr (Acts 7:57). He witnessed and approved this brutal killing of a great deacon. He hated Christian faith and persecuted Christians without mercy because he believed the Christian movement was a threat to Judaism. He got a permission to travel to

Damascus to capture Christians and bring them to Jerusalem to have them persecuted. God stopped him in his tracks on the Damascus road. Mr. Saul (Paul) was a human. We, like him, had done terrible things before the gracious salvation of our Lord Jesus. We, like him, our life is the sum of victories and failures, and our personality a mixture of strengths and weaknesses.

Being an honest book, the Bible presents Paul, its greatest Apostle just as he is, with weaknesses as well as strength, with victories as well as failures. In fact, it does with every one of its great characters. Adam was a perfect man but he had weaknesses too. He teamed up with Eve to bring sin into the world. Noah was a godly man whose godliness saved him and his family from the flood, but he became drunk and embarrassed himself in front of his sons. Abraham's faith was counted as righteousness and made him the founder of the Jewish nation, but under direct pressure, he distorted the truth about his wife. Sarah became the mother of a nation and an ancestor of Jesus, a first woman listed in the Hall of Faith. But attempted to work problems in her family out on her own, without consulting God. She had trouble believing God's promises to her. Moses was the meekest Jewish leader, but he failed to enter the promise land because of disobedience. Samuel was the last faithful and most effective of Israel's judges, but failed to lead his sons into a close relationship with God. David was a man after God's own heart, but he committed adultery with Bathsheba and orchestrated a murder of Uriah, Bathsheba's husband. Solomon became known as the wisest man who ever lived, but allowed his wives to affect his loyalty with God. Job is a supreme example of faithfulness and a model of trust, but even he had to repent of some reckless words.

Peter was one of the three in the core group of disciples and the only one to identify Jesus as Messiah. He was the first great voice of the gospel during and after Pentecost, but he often spoke without thinking (impulsive). And during Jesus' trial, he denied three times that he knew him. James was the ambitious man deeply committed to Jesus, the first of the 12 apostles to be killed for his faith, but struggled with a hot temper and judgmental spirit (Luke 9:54) and selfishness (Mark 10:37). John was one of the three closest to Jesus, a man who wrote five New Testament books: the Gospel of John, 1, 2, 3 Epistles of John, and Revelation. But along with James, shared a tendency to outbursts of anger and selfishness. The list goes on. In every case, including Paul's, great men and women of God failed the Lord because of their imperfections and glaring weaknesses. In fact, there is only one perfect Person who ever lived – Jesus. Brené says "Imperfections are not inadequacies, they are reminders that we're all in this together." I believe that this contingent of great men and women of faith were aware of this fact. They won the crown of glory simply because they kept pressing on toward the goal despite their inescapable weaknesses. They had some great strengths of character, but they have also done foolish things, lived foolishly, but they learned not to relive the past.

We have also done things of which we are ashamed, and we continue to live in the tension of what we have been and what we want to be. Because our hope is in Christ, however, we can let go of past guilt and look forward to what God will help us become. Do not dwell on your past. In my study, I came across a saying that, "When God changes a life; he does not take away personality characteristics, but puts them to effective use in his service." When I read this, I found a reason why God continued to use those great believers (admittedly, stronger than most of us) even with their scars and failures and shortcomings. However, God's willingness to use them depended upon their resilience, and resilience that came from repentance and discovery of the internal ability to deal with past failures. Paul tells us that the secret of dealing with our past is in doing one thing – forgetting the past. We need to start realising that God is willing to forgive and forget our past; we then need to move on to a life of faith, obedience and service. We need to look forward to a fuller and more meaningful life because our hope is in Christ.

THINGS TO FORGET: LESSONS FROM PAUL'S EXPERIENCES

Like all of us, through his entire life, Apostle Paul was subjected to injustice, betrayal, trauma, and heartbreaks. All these things, he resolved to forget. Drawing inferences from some interesting passages of his books, I was able to classify these 'must-forget' things into three categories. These things could have hindered Paul in his pursuit of a heavenly prize.

Struggles and Failures

I have never seen a leader that is able to identify with the struggles and failures of ordinary men and women like Paul (Romans 7). Interestingly, unlike most leaders, he admits that he is like them in their struggles. He says, "For I know that nothing good lives in me, that is, in my flesh [my human nature, my worldliness – my sinful capacity]. For the willingness [to do good] is present in me, but the doing of good is not. For the good that I want to do, I do not do, but I practice the very evil that I do not want. But if I am doing the very thing that I do not want to do, I am no longer the one doing it [that is, it is not me that acts], but the sin [nature] which lives in me" (Romans 7:18-20). What a struggle! What a conflict of two natures! The Christian life is a struggle. The Christian life is a constant war. Even with our spiritual nature being reborn through Jesus, we still experience a constant conflict between the spiritual and the human nature. The conflict that often leads to inner wretchedness and struggle for peace. I remember how I used to struggle with fiery temper. The Bible has a lot to say about the importance of controlling one's temper. It is important to note that anger itself is not sinful. It is a valid emotion, but the Bible warns, "In your anger do not sin." (Ephesians 4:26). God's Word here teaches that giving in to one's temper is a sin. Midway through 1999, my tendency to lose temper led me to sin. One minute I was full of rage and the next I was crying and sad because I had done something foolish - I violently slapped, hit and kicked someone. I felt screwed up. I let God down. I acted foolishly. Indeed, "...he who is quick-tempered exposes and exalts his foolishness [for all to see] (Proverbs 14:29b). I exposed my foolishness. We may often feel justified in losing our temper, particularly when someone has hurt or offended us. But, we must always know that although all sin is forgivable, ultimately, no sin is justifiable. When we have sinned because we lashed out in anger and hurt others, we must repent unconditionally. This is exactly what I did – Asked for forgiveness.

During one of our interdenominational churches' Christmas conferences, Pastor Jerry Masedi offered an intriguing comment on Matthew 4:19. He said, "Change is a process. In the process of following Jesus, Jesus makes us." He implied that Jesus transforms our imperfections while we follow him. He emphasised that being born again takes a moment of faith, but becoming like Christ is a lifelong process. He said we become like him in the process of following. He then went on to disclose that he used to struggle with a terrible anger. He recalled how he one day went into a rage so he ended shouting at his parents and siblings as he released his anger. Worse still, his anger overwhelmed him that he opened the house, took a bag of maize meal, and emptied it to the ground. What an outrageous act! But seeing how he has matured with time, you would easily be tempted to think he had never struggled with serious issues (anger and short-temper) in his life. I always compare the Christian life with a strenuous fight. We get knocked down sometimes, but we become better, wiser and stronger when we rise again. We rise again when we confess sins caused by our failure to overcome momentous struggles. The only deliverance comes through Jesus our Saviour.

What are you struggling with? Are you even embarrassed to expose some of your struggles and failures? You are not alone in this, I still feel uncomfortable to disclose some of the humiliating moments of defeats in my life. Most of these occurred while I was still a teenager and meanwhile some happened when I was still spiritually immature. Like Paul, in all these struggles I felt trapped (7:14), confused (7:15), and frustrated (7:24). Eagerness to do what is right was there but unable to follow through (7:18). Thus, Paul reveals that he found himself failing in ways that weren't even attractive to him. However, he tells us that when struggle results in failure, we must learn to depend totally on the work of Christ for salvation. Depending on Jesus' grace allows us to forget our failures. It allows us to move forward with confidence, leaving self-doubt and letdowns in the past. One of the lifelong lessons I gained in the past eighteen years of ministry is that we don't learn any new lessons from agonising over our failures. I have learnt to let my failures fall by the wayside and move forward. Paul resolved to forget what is behind him and move towards the goal. Because he was moving forward, he did not want to take the painful memories with him. I know there are memories that grow us. But we need to leave behind those memories that aren't going to grow us.

Criticisms and Traumas

Aristotle said, "Criticism is something you can avoid easily – by saying nothing, doing nothing, and being nothing." Yet, criticism has a far-reaching effect in our lives. In 2 Corinthians 11:23- 12:10, Paul tells us about the traumas caused by excessive criticism by his own church members. The Corinthians had criticised him for his supposed weakness. His opponents had also criticised his claim to be an apostle saying he had not experienced visions and revelations. John C Maxwell says, "The price of leadership is criticism." However, criticism is not an easy thing to bear. It traumatises you. What actually traumatised Paul was the fact that he was gradually losing credibility in the eyes of many Corinthians. In leadership, you can lose everything, but you cannot afford to lose credibility. John C Maxwell says that "When leaders surrender their credibility, they lose the right to lead" (The Maxwell Leadership Bible). Thus, Apostle Paul took this seriously. Although his approach was questionable and foolish, he felt obliged to do something about the criticisms. At the outset, he asks his readers to receive him even as a fool, so that he may boast a little. He knew that self-confident boasting is worldly and foolish. But in the circumstances where his converts have been swayed by the boasting of others (false apostles), he felt compelled to boast a little himself.

This is what trauma does to leaders; it pushes them over the edge, making them resort to 'foolish speech' to handle criticism. To get back at their critics, traumatised ministers often review their track record in the ministry. Oftentimes, when you hear a minister reminding people about how the ministry begun, boasting about his or her own accomplishments, visions and revelations he or she has received from the Lord, that minister is traumatised. I am not immune from this. I did it many times under the pretence that I have been bold and emphatic. But, like Paul, I know it is the 'foolish' way to handle criticism. Well, maybe sometimes this approach is right, while at other times it is best to wait.

When it comes to boasting, first Paul claims he is better servant of Christ than the other apostles (false) because he had suffered far more than they have in the ministry. To support his claim, he provided a list of his apostolic trials which can be divided into three major categories or sections: imprisonments, beatings and being near death, frequent journeys, with description of the dangers of travel, and toil and hardship, with an account of the privations involved in these. Second, Paul goes on to boast about his visions and revelations. Of the many visions and revelations he had experienced, Paul singles the most awe-inspiring one, the one that occurred fourteen years ago. He singled this vision simply because by claiming such an experience could completely outflank and outsmart his opponents. He says he was caught up to the third heaven, to paradise where he heard unspeakable things. He disclosed the bare facts about his experiences in order to meet the criticism of his opponents, to silence them. He was traumatised by the criticism of the church. We can now see why he said, "I focus on this one thing: Forgetting the past and looking forward to what lies ahead." He suffered so much injustice that he had to forget in order to win the prize. He had to forget the labels that have been placed on him by his opponents. Like Paul, many of us have labels placed on us by the world around us, making us feel weak and stigmatised. We have shed so many skin cells, so many old lives, in all of the days that have passed. To press on to reach the end of the race and to receive the heavenly prize, we need to forget all the traumas of the past.

Heartbreaks and Headaches

The saying "When days are dark, friends are few" is entirely true. When the world has turned dark, friends run away from you. Your own friends look at you as a stranger. You have no shoulder to cry on, and this breaks your heart. During the final days of his life, Paul was abound in chains in a Roman cell, awaiting his appeal to Caesar, and ultimately his own execution. He suffered physical distress. He was in great need, he needed friends, but almost everyone else deserted him. He was lonely, needy and trying very hard to be faithful in the most difficult of circumstances. Thus, he writes to Timothy, "As you know, everyone in the province of Asia has deserted me – even Phygelus and Hermogenes. May the Lord show special kindness to Onesiphorus and all his family because he often visited and encouraged me. He was never ashamed of me because I was in chains" (2 Timothy 1:15-18).

This period of bondage was quite difficult for Paul. This was his final imprisonment that took place in the "Well-Dungeon" near the capital, a damp and cold vaulted pit. It was very cold that he appealed to Timothy to bring his cloak and to do his best to come before winter sets in (2 Timothy 4: 13, 21). His own partners and friends forsook him because they were ashamed of his chains. They did not want to associate themselves with a convicted criminal. This broke his heart. He spent the nights crying on the floor of the cold well dungeon. During these dark days of loneliness, discomfort, disappointment, and uncertainty, he needed friends, but his friends betrayed him.

In 2014, I preached on the sermon titled, '7 people leaders know they can count on'. I said leaders could count on someone who is not ashamed of their chains. I preached about

51

a man named Onesiphorus, a man whose presence provided strength and renewal Paul needed. Like many Biblical names, Onesiphorus holds significance. Onesiphorus means "profit-bringer". This man came in when everyone else got out. Pastors need profit-bringers not pain-bringers in their ministries. Profit-bringers just do not care how much you have blundered in your ministry; they stick with you through thick and thin. We cannot easily fulfill God-given vision without these men and women on our side.

Between the years 1999 and 2002, rumours broke out about me and many who believed it turned against me. As the rumour spread, my credibility as a preacher was directly affected. Having rumours spread about you is hurtful and unsettling knowing that people are talking about you behind your back. I normally prefer not to respond to the rumour. I believe responding to a rumour dignifies a rumour. But the silence tortured me emotionally and caused an unexplainable pain in my heart. During these trying times, I needed profit-bringers. God being a caring Father, he sent three friends in my life, Pastor Peter Mahasha, Mr. Doctor Malatji, and Pastor Freddy Mogale who continued to encourage me. They were profit-bringers in my life and ministry. Their support made me come out of that situation stronger, wiser, and more resilient.

Do you see why it is important to forget about the betrayal by friends and abandonment by pastors we once trusted? Paul urges us to forget about the people who let us down. He urges us to forget about the swords that swiftly stepped us in the back, about the broken promises and shattered trust. He urges us to forget and move on with life. We cannot let the past betrayals make us bitter. Paul forgot about it, so let us do the same.